T R

D0533750

HARRISON, Paul

The Cold War

W
FRANKLIN WATTS

First published in 2005 by Franklin Watts
Reprinted 2007

Copyright © 2005 Arcturus Publishing Limited

Franklin Watts
338 Euston Road, London, NW1 3BH

Franklin Watts Australia
Level 17/207 Kent Street, Sydney, NSW 2000

Produced by Arcturus Publishing Limited
26/27 Bickels Yard, 151–153 Bermondsey Street
London SE1 3HA

Series concept: Alex Woolf
Editor: Philip de Ste. Croix
Designer: Stonecastle Graphics
Picture researcher: Thomas Mitchell

Picture credits:
All the photographs in this book were supplied by
Getty Images and are reproduced here with their
permission. The photographs appearing on the pages
listed below are Time Life images.
Time Life Pictures/Getty Images: 27, 38, 39, 40, 42,
43, 44.

A CIP catalogue record for this book is available
from the British Library

Dewey Decimal Classification Number: 909.82'5

ISBN: 978-0-7496-7720-6

Printed in China

Franklin Watts is a division of
Hachette Children's Books

Contents

1 The Origins of the Cold War

In the 1950s schoolchildren in the United States routinely took part in defence drills to practise what they should do in the event of a nuclear attack on their town. The advice to 'duck and cover' (or duck under a desk and roll into a ball facing away from the window) would actually have been futile, but the possibility of attack was genuine enough. This was the reality of the Cold War – a conflict that lasted for nearly 50 years, that changed countries and put the planet itself under threat. The way we live our lives today has been shaped by the events that unfolded during this period.

American schoolchildren practise the duck and cover procedure. In the 1950s a film called *Duck and Cover* encouraged Americans to be alert to the possibility of nuclear attack. This was part of the civil defence policy – a range of measures aimed at protecting the general public.

The Cold War was a global conflict between the West and the East, predominantly the United States and the Union of Soviet Socialist Republics (USSR) or Soviet Union. These were the two major world powers – or 'superpowers' as they came to be known. However, neither side fought the other directly, so the antagonism was called a 'cold' war. If the two power blocs had fought each other with their armed forces, it would have been a 'hot' war. Each side viewed the other with intense suspicion and fear.

Some historians trace the start of the Cold War to the ill-feeling that existed between East and West in 1918 when the USA and Britain sent troops to Russia to help in the fight against the newly formed

VOICES FROM THE PAST

The Allied leaders

Despite their disagreements in Yalta and Potsdam, the Western allied leaders respected Stalin. Churchill described the Soviet leader as:

'*...this truly great man, the father of his nation.*'

Although Stalin remained wary of the Western leaders, he could still separate personal and political feelings. After visiting an ailing Roosevelt, who suffered from poliomyelitis, he said to an aide:

'*Why did nature have to punish him so? Is he any worse than other people?*'

Both quoted in Simon Sebag Montefiore, *Stalin: The Court of the Red Tsar* (Phoenix, 2003)

British troops stand next to bomb-damaged trains in northern Russia in 1919. Between 1918–1920 Russia was caught up in a vicious civil war. The United States and Britain helped the 'White Russians', the rebel group fighting against the 'Red Russians', the Bolshevik communist government headed by Vladimir Ilyich Lenin. The communist forces held on to power.

communist government there. However, most people trace the start of the Cold War to 1945. As the Second World War (1939–45) ended, the Allied leaders – US president Franklin D. Roosevelt, British prime minister Winston Churchill and Soviet premier Joseph Stalin – met to discuss the final stages of the campaign and how the defeated European countries would be governed after the war.

Adolf Hitler salutes his troops during the occupation of Poland in September 1939. The German army had twice tried to invade Russia, as had Napoleon's French troops a century earlier. It was against such invasion attempts that the USSR sought to protect itself at the conclusion of the Second World War.

The Yalta Conference

This meeting took place in February 1945 in the Soviet town of Yalta on the Crimean Peninsula. War was still raging in Europe and the Pacific, and the Allied leaders discussed how to defeat the Germans and Japanese and how the world would be realigned when the war was over. The United States and Britain wanted the USSR to send troops to help fight Japan, which Stalin agreed to. Next on the agenda was the formation of the United Nations (UN), an international organization of countries established to work for world peace and security. The Soviet Union was worried that the other two Allies might join forces against it in the UN to promote policies that served their own purposes, so it was agreed that each of the major powers would have the right of veto. The leaders also agreed that Germany would be split into four zones of occupation with each of their countries, along with France, taking control of one section. The final issue was Poland.

The Soviet Union had been invaded through Poland twice in the space of thirty years and it wanted to safeguard against this happening again. A decision was taken to move the Soviet border with Poland westwards to give the USSR more territory while Poland in turn would take territory from Germany. The USSR agreed that Poland would be allowed to hold free elections rather than stay under Soviet control.

While the Yalta Conference had seemingly gone well, there were signs of deeper, underlying tensions. These became more apparent when the allies met at Potsdam near the German capital, Berlin, in July 1945. The war in Europe was over – the Soviets had entered Berlin from the east, while the US and British forces had closed in from the west. By this time Roosevelt had died and he had been replaced as US president by Harry Truman. During the conference the Conservative Party was defeated in the British general election, and Churchill was replaced as prime minister by Labour Party leader Clement Attlee.

The Question of Reparations

Although the Potsdam Conference settled the division of Germany, there were other areas of disagreement including the precise border between Russia and Poland. The other main sticking point was the payment of reparations by Germany. The US and Britain wanted Germany to be economically stable before it was made to pay reparations; the USSR wanted its payments immediately. Stalin pointed out that over 27 million Soviet citizens had died in the war and he was in no mood to help Germany recover. Finally a decision was taken that the USSR would have its reparations immediately while the other Allies would wait. The leaders had reached in agreement, but there was no trust between them. East and West were wary of each other's motives and of what might happen in the future.

Clement Attlee (left), Harry Truman (centre) and Joseph Stalin pose for the cameras during the Potsdam Conference in 1945. The change in western personnel disappointed Stalin. He thought Churchill to be an impressive leader and preferred Roosevelt to Truman. This may have been because Truman took a harder line with Stalin than Roosevelt had done.

TURNING POINT

How Europe was divided

The final division of Europe agreed to at the Potsdam Conference was partly based on a hastily scribbled plan that Churchill had written on a piece of paper and shown to Stalin. The Soviet leader studied the plan for a few moments and drew a big tick next to it to signify that he agreed with it. General agreement on the fate of Europe had been decided in a few short minutes. Essentially the Soviets were to be left in control of the countries that their Red Army had liberated during the war and the Western allies would look after the rest. This arrangement was intended to be temporary; elections were supposed to be held later to decide the fate of the occupied countries democratically. However, events were to take a very different course to the one anticipated by the Allies.

The West suspected that the USSR was planning to build a communist empire. At the end of the war the USSR controlled a large part of Europe, namely Poland, Czechoslovakia, Hungary, Romania, Bulgaria and Albania. It installed governments there that were in broad agreement with the Soviet political system. The West's fears were confirmed when the free elections in Poland, promised by Stalin at Yalta, voted in a communist majority which then began to suppress non-communists. By 1948, the USSR was in control of Eastern Europe. There was a clear division between East and West. As Winston Churchill famously described it in a speech delivered in Fulton, Missouri in 1946: 'an iron curtain has descended across the continent'.

Just as alarming for the USA was the state that Europe was in. While the war had actually improved the US economy, by 1945 Europe lay literally in ruins. This presented a two-fold problem. Firstly, communism seems very attractive to people who have nothing, and the United States did not want communism to spread its influence any further. Secondly, the poor economic state of America's allies prevented them from helping in the struggle against communism. This was particularly true of Britain, which found itself unable to continue funding the non-communist side fighting in the civil war raging in Greece. If Britain pulled out, the communist forces would probably win. This prospect pushed the United States into implementing two momentous policies.

The first of these is known as the Truman Doctrine. In 1947 Truman went before Congress to ask for $400 million to help the anti-communist forces in the Greek Civil War. Truman also proposed that the United States should lend money to any country that needed help to fight communism. Congress approved the proposal and aid was sent to the anti-communist Greek forces and neighbouring Turkey, which was also threatened with a communist takeover.

Truman's proposal was fleshed out by the Marshall Plan, named after General George Marshall, the US secretary of state. This aid package helped the fight against communism by offering financial aid to help European countries rebuild themselves. Aid was not restricted to non-communist countries; communist governments were offered assistance too. However, the USSR rejected this offer, which it viewed with deep suspicion. The Marshall Plan helped drive the former allies further apart.

The Marshall Plan was not the only economic policy to cause a rift between East and West. The issue of a new German currency brought the old allies to the brink of war. At the end of the Second World War,

In 1945 the German city of Dresden lay in ruins. Many of Europe's cities were heavily damaged during the war, leading to problems such as homelessness, disease and starvation. This perilous situation was of grave concern to Europe and the USA alike.

TURNING POINT

The Marshall Plan

The Marshall Plan was a lifeline for many European nations. Although the war was over, its legacy still bit deep into countries devastated by the conflict. In Britain, rationing was still in force and the supply situation was getting worse. In France there was a real threat of a disgruntled population backing the communists, and communist militants were actively stirring up industrial unrest. To make matters worse, Europe was hit by a particularly harsh winter in 1947 and suffered a poor annual harvest. Without the help of the Marshall Plan, Europe's recovery would have taken far longer and its political future would have been more unpredictable.

The Marshall Plan gets under way as a consignment of sugar arrives in Britain in 1949. American food and equipment was a literal life-saver for the impoverished citizens of many European countries. Although the USSR turned down the offer of aid, the communist country of Yugoslavia did accept some American help.

Germany and its capital city, Berlin, had been split into four zones. Each zone was under the control of one country: the USA, Britain, France or the USSR. Berlin itself lay deep inside East Germany, the part of the country that was controlled by the USSR. The United States and Britain were resolved that the German recovery should be swift, a stance vigorously opposed by the USSR, which feared a strong Germany.

A City Divided

In 1947 the Western allies joined their zones to form Trizonia. In 1948 the allies also agreed to replace the reichsmark – the old, now worthless German currency – with a new deutschmark to speed economic recovery. The Soviet Union objected, fearing the formation of a powerful West Germany, and retaliated by introducing the ostmark in East Germany, claiming that this should be the new German currency. The allies declared the ostmark to be invalid in Berlin and introduced a special version of the deutschmark, called the B-mark, to the capital.

In 1949 the city of Berlin was split into four different sectors. Initially there was little difficulty in moving from one sector to another. However, as Cold War tensions increased, the citizens of Berlin eventually found themselves trapped in their war-damaged city, caught up in a political stand-off between East and West.

Stalin responded by closing all land links from West Germany to Berlin. The city was cut off from the West. It looked as if West Berlin would be starved into submission. Some of the allies suggested that the blockade should be broken by force, but the USA was unwilling to risk war. The British air force, on the other hand, had a more unusual plan – it suggested flying in supplies. The plan seemed unlikely to succeed. Nothing like it had been attempted before, the organization would be difficult to coordinate and the costs would be high. Nevertheless the US and British governments decided to give it a try.

Bringing in supplies by air became a round-the-clock operation. At one point transport planes were landing in Berlin every ninety seconds. By spring 1949 aircraft brought in around 8,000 tonnes of supplies every day. Although Soviet fighter planes buzzed the transport aircraft, they were unwilling to provoke an armed conflict. By May 1949, it was obvious that the

DER SEKTOR DER FREIHEIT
USST DIE KÄMPFER FÜR FREIHEIT UND RECHT DER WESTSEKTOREN!

YOU ARE LEAVING
THE AMERICAN SECTOR
ВЫ ВЫЕЗЖАЕТЕ ИЗ
АМЕРИКАНСКОЙ ЗОНЫ
VOUS SORTEZ
DU SECTEUR AMERICAIN

An American supply plane flies into Berlin during the blockade when Stalin closed all land links between West Germany and the city. The airlift was a triumph of organization and provided the West with a means of breaking the blockade without having to use military force.

VOICES FROM THE PAST

The formation of NATO

In 1949 eleven European countries plus the United States formed the North Atlantic Treaty Organization (NATO) to implement the recently signed North Atlantic Treaty. Under the terms of the treaty, if any member state was attacked by the Soviets, the other nations would come to its aid. NATO was established to help to secure peace in Europe and maintain close ties between Europe and America. Lord Ismay, NATO's first secretary-general, summed up NATO's purpose in this way:

'To keep the Russians out, the Americans in and the Germans down.'

Lord Ismay quoted on the Peace Pledge Union website
www.ppu.org.uk/peacematters/1999/pm_99sp_nato.html

blockade of Berlin would not work. On 12 May Stalin called the blockade off. The West had defeated the USSR without firing a shot.

Throughout all his dealings with Stalin, Truman believed he had a distinct advantage – America had the atomic bomb, the Soviets did not. The first A-bomb, dropped on 6 August 1945 during the Second World War, devastated the Japanese city of Hiroshima. Just one bomb killed over 100,000 people and made many more seriously ill from radiation sickness. Never before had the world seen such a powerful weapon of mass destruction.

The Manhattan Project

The atomic bomb had been developed in secret as part of an initiative codenamed the Manhattan Project. Truman told Stalin at the Potsdam Conference that he had a secret weapon and took Stalin's lack of reaction as indicating that the Soviet leader did not understand what he was talking about. In fact, Stalin was all too aware of what Truman meant, for the simple reason that Soviet spies had been passing information about the Manhattan Project directly to Moscow.

At the time of the Berlin blockade, the United States was still the only nation with the bomb. However this all changed three months after the blockade ended – in August the USSR tested its first bomb. America was shocked. Its leaders knew the Soviets had been

J. Robert Oppenheimer (left), one of the creators of the atomic bomb, is pictured with other senior members of the Manhattan Project. The photograph at which Oppenheimer is pointing shows the explosion of the second atom bomb to be dropped on Japan during the Second World War. The bomb was detonated over the city of Nagasaki on 9 August 1945.

developing a bomb, but believed that they were years away from a successful test. The arms race had begun.

From this point onwards the USA and the Soviet Union competed to construct more powerful and larger stockpiles of weapons. A more destructive hydrogen bomb, which was 1,000 times more powerful than the Hiroshima atomic bomb, was developed in 1952. By 1957 intercontinental ballistic missiles (ICBMs) were being tested. These long-range missiles could be launched from one continent to strike a target in another. The missiles were followed by the development of US submarines that could launch nuclear missiles from beneath the surface of the ocean.

A general pattern began to emerge – the US concentrated on developing better weapons, while the USSR focussed on the sheer quantity of missiles it could produce. Soon, enough weapons existed to destroy all life on earth. The superpowers were locked in an expensive battle for supremacy which cast a long shadow over the Cold War.

The Americans test an ICBM in 1960. The capabilities of ICBMs to travel huge distances changed the face of modern warfare for ever. The missile in the photograph was launched using an Atlas rocket – these rockets would later be used to carry astronauts into space.

HOW DID IT HAPPEN?

Who was responsible for the Cold War?

The arms race was a physical demonstration of how the Cold War was escalating. Historians disagree over who was responsible for provoking this increasingly serious conflict. Some blame the Soviets. The British commentator Paul Johnson wrote: 'In effect Stalin had polarized the earth … It was he who had built the Iron Curtain … (he) hated "Westerners" in the same way Hitler hated Jews.'

Others blame the Americans, amongst them the historian Eric Hobsbawm: 'Among democratic countries it was only in the USA that presidents were elected against communism … In fact, as the rhetoric of J.F. Kennedy's electioneering demonstrates … the issue was not the academic threat of communist world domination, but the maintenance of a real US supremacy.'

Paul Johnson, *Modern Times – A History of the World from the 1920s to the 1990s* (Weidenfield & Nicholson, 1983); Eric Hobsbawm, *Age of Extremes, The Short Twentieth Century 1914–1991* (Michael Joseph, 1994)

2 The Cold War Freezes

The Cold War was not just a European confrontation. While East and West clashed over Berlin, the war took a more dramatic course in Asia. At the end of the Second World War the north of Korea had been occupied by Soviet forces, while the US took control of the South. At Potsdam the two countries agreed to split the country; the dividing line was drawn at the latitude known as the 38th parallel. They also agreed to hold elections to unite the country. In 1949 the United States pulled its troops out of South Korea.

American troops land at Inchon in South Korea on 15 September 1950 during the first year of the Korean War. The invasion was a bold gamble, but hugely successful. The capital city, Seoul, was liberated and the North Korean army was quickly pushed back over the 38th parallel.

However, the elections never happened. In June 1950, with US military forces gone and with Soviet approval, North Korea invaded the South. North Korean troops rapidly occupied the South's capital, Seoul, which fell on 28 June, and advanced rapidly to occupy most of the country. US troops, led by General Douglas MacArthur and operating as part of a combined United Nations force, landed in South Korea and led a spirited counterattack. They pushed the communist troops back over the 38th parallel. MacArthur's men continued to advance northwards, capturing the North's capital, Pyongyang, on 12 October 1950, and forcing the North Korean troops back towards the Yalu River, the Korean border with China.

VOICES FROM THE PAST

The Korean War

The Korean War is often called the forgotten war. The US Korean war veteran Ray L. Walker explains:

'As far as the American public was concerned, Korea was an unknown land of little importance ... It is also important to note that the Korean War is the first war America did not win an ultimate victory ... At the end of the war there was merely a sigh of relief in America. There were no parades, no show of national pride or support for the veterans. We just came home, and when discharged we went about building our lives.'

Ray L. Walker, quoted on the Korean War Veterans National Museum and Library website, www.theforgottenvictory.org

US troops huddle in their trenches under bombardment from the North Korean army. By the end of the war the conflict had begun to resemble the First World War with troops on both sides dug into static positions and few gains being made by either side.

This had the unwelcome effect of bringing China, another communist country, into the conflict. The Chinese were unwilling to allow fellow communists to suffer foreign aggression so close to China's borders. They sent troops to help. The Soviets, always wary of provoking war, would not commit troops, but they did supply military hardware. However, they expected payment for it – much to the disgust of the Chinese. The Soviet Union and China were both communist powers, but they regarded one another with great mutual distrust.

For its part, the United States did not want to go to war with China. In reality it did not have much choice. The UN forces had been driven back beyond the 38th parallel by the sheer numbers of Chinese and Korean troops. UN troops fought back in 1951, regaining lost ground and by July 1951 both sides were dug in along a line just north of the 38th parallel. Stalemate followed. Eventually, in 1953, a ceasefire was agreed, but for three years the Cold War had briefly turned hot.

The formation of the KGB

Formed in 1954, but with its origins stretching back to the Russian Revolution, the KGB (*Komitet Gosudarstvennoy Bezopasnosti* or Committee for State Security) was a secret police organization in charge of national security in the Soviet Union. The formation of the KGB heralded a new approach to spying and national security. One organization now controlled and co-ordinated activities such as the running of the secret police, propaganda, catching enemy spies, and dealing with any internal political, religious or social dissent. The KGB was a powerful force – a clear indication of the importance that the superpowers placed on the dark arts of espionage.

Ethel and Julius Rosenberg on the way to prison in 1951. The couple were convicted of spying for the USSR, and in particular of revealing atomic secrets. The pair were executed by electric chair in June 1953 – the only Americans to be executed for spying during the Cold War.

Espionage and Counter-espionage

The outbreak of the Korean War had caught America by surprise, partly because the US intelligence-gathering organization, the Central Intelligence Agency (CIA), had failed to predict it. This served to highlight how important a role the rival spy networks played in the Cold War. Both East and West spent vast amounts of time and money trying to discover what the other side was doing. Spying became one of the main areas of conflict in the Cold War.

Of course, spying was not a new activity. Throughout history most countries have spied on other nations in some way or another. Spying often involved an agent in a foreign country reporting back any significant information that he or she could discover. This was how the Soviets had originally learned about the US atomic bomb programme. What made the Cold War so significant was that the technology of espionage progressed very rapidly in this period.

During the Cold War scientists developed a range of special equipment for secret agents. Listening devices, tape recorders and cameras were supplied to spies. Much of this equipment was miniaturized, as easy concealment was vital. Agents were also given more lethal equipment: guns that could be concealed inside cigarette lighters or newspapers, suicide pills, and in one instance a poison-tipped umbrella.

MISSILE TRANSPORTERS

12 PROB GUIDELINE MISSILES

HEAVY EQUIPMENT

5 MISSILE DOLLIES

20 LONG CYLINDRICAL TANKS

MISSILE TRANSPORTERS

Although planting spies in an enemy's country could be an effective way of gathering information, it was also unpredictable. If an agent was captured or killed, the flow of information was lost. It was also expensive and time-consuming to train and equip agents. As the Cold War unfolded, technology became more important as machinery replaced the need for lots of agents on the ground.

Eyes in the Sky

A good example of this new type of intelligence-gathering was the U2 spy plane – a US-developed aircraft that took photographs from a very high altitude. By flying high, it kept out of the range of Soviet fighters and anti-aircraft missiles. In time these aircraft were replaced by even more sophisticated technology. Spy satellites circled the Earth. They were able to listen in to conversations or relay back pictures so clear that even newspaper headlines could be read from space.

Advances in spying technology continued with the development of stealth technology – a way of making aircraft and even ships invisible to radar. Within the span of the Cold War, the art of spying evolved remarkably – from an individual sending secret messages to making aircraft 'disappear'.

This photograph of a Soviet missile site on the island of Cuba was taken by an American U2 spy plane in October 1962. This evidence of the presence of Soviet ballistic missiles in Cuba led to one of the most serious confrontations between the United States and the Soviet Union during the Cold War.

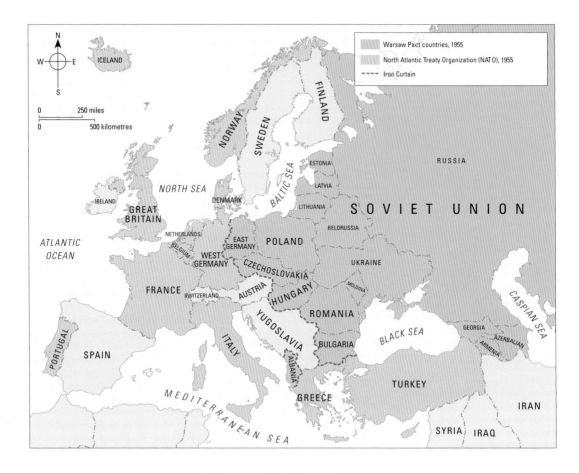

Europe during the 1950s when the NATO alliance confronted the Warsaw Pact countries. East and West were clearly divided with Eastern Europe effectively sealed off by a line of communist-controlled countries. Winston Churchill famously described this dividing line as the 'Iron Curtain'.

The USSR after Stalin

In the Soviet Union, Joseph Stalin used a network of spies and informers, not only against the West, but also to hunt down opposition at home. Stalin's power was absolute and he ruled with an iron fist. Trade unions and religions were effectively banned; as was any other opposition, social or political.

Stalin's need for total control also drove a wedge between Yugoslavia and the USSR. Although Yugoslavia was a communist country, it was not under the direct influence of the USSR. However, Stalin believed that all communist governments should do as he commanded. When Marshal Tito, the Yugoslav leader, refused to do as Stalin ordered, all diplomatic relations were broken off with Yugoslavia.

Stalin died in March 1953. His death left a power vacuum that was eventually filled by Nikita Khrushchev. Khrushchev's appointment as first secretary of the Soviet Communist Party seemed about to usher in a new period of freedom. In 1956 he criticized some of the harsher aspects of Stalin's reign at the Twentieth Congress of the Communist Party of the Soviet Union. He also restored relations with Yugoslavia.

TURNING POINT

The Warsaw Pact

In 1955, worried about the power of the West's NATO alliance, most of the Eastern European communist nations (Albania, Bulgaria, Czechoslovakia, East Germany, Hungary, Poland, Romania and the USSR) bound themselves together by signing a treaty called the Warsaw Pact. All members were committed to giving assistance to any other member that was attacked in Europe. The Eastern bloc was now, formally, a united military presence capable of confronting NATO head on.

Khrushchev's more relaxed approach to government was tested in Poland where strikes against wage cuts quickly turned into general protest against communist control. The authorities mobilized troops with tanks to crush the protest violently. However, Khrushchev did make some economic concessions. He also appointed Wladyslaw Gomulka as head of the government. Gomulka was a friend of Marshal Tito, and he had previously been imprisoned by Stalin. Gomulka's appointment felt like a move away from the oppressive Soviet rule of old.

These events caught the attention of fellow communists in Hungary. Riots broke out there in support of the Poles. Hungary wanted to leave the Warsaw Pact and become independent. Khrushchev could not allow splits to develop on his side of the Iron Curtain, so a combination of Soviet and Hungarian troops put down the uprising. As in Poland a popular politician, Imre Nagy, was then appointed new leader of the communist party.

Although troops withdrew from Hungary, the mood in the capital, Budapest, was still ugly. Workers seized public buildings, new political parties were formed and free elections were held in some parts of the country. Nagy condoned these actions and went as far as to form a coalition government with some of the new parties. Finally, on 1 November, Nagy declared Hungary to be neutral and no longer under Soviet control.

This was a step too far for Khrushchev. Thousands of Soviet troops and tanks invaded Budapest and eight days of vicious street fighting followed. Hungary appealed to the US for help, but again America was unwilling to

Soviet tanks patrol the streets of Budapest, Hungary in November 1956. Street-fighting flared around the Hungarian capital as the Soviet troops moved in to put down the revolution, but the Hungarian people had little chance against such overpowering armour.

confront the USSR head on. The uprising was crushed. Between 3,000 and 4,000 Hungarians died and many more fled the country. Nagy was arrested and executed. Hungary was not to be free.

The Space Race

As events in Hungary showed, the United States and the USSR were unwilling to confront one another militarily, but there were other ways in which they could battle for supremacy. This was shown when both superpowers strove to be the first to conquer space itself. This most futuristic of conflicts had its roots in the Second World War when Germany had shelled Britain with V1 and V2 long-range rockets. The advantages of this type of warfare were clear – a country could destroy enemy targets without endangering its own aircraft or pilots. When the war was over, both the USSR and the United States encouraged German rocket scientists to work for them to take advantage of their knowledge of rocket technology.

The reasons for doing this were twofold. The military uses were obvious, but each of the superpowers also wanted to prove to the world that its political system was the best. Harnessing the potential of rocket technology to launch a space vehicle was an ideal way for a country to show its superiority. The USSR took an early lead in this race to explore space – on 4 October 1957 it launched the world's first satellite, Sputnik 1, into orbit around the Earth.

It was a very simple craft, but it was Earth's first spaceship and it grabbed the world's attention. Around 56 cm in diameter, Sputnik contained a radio transmitter which sent back a beeping signal so that scientists on Earth could track its progress. Ordinary people could tune in their radios and hear it as it sped overhead. Basic as Sputnik was, it alarmed America. Russia had reached space first – this was a great blow to national pride. Also, if a rocket could successfully launch a satellite into space, it was also reasonable to assume that a rocket could now drop a warhead on the United States.

The Soviet Union's early lead was extended when Yuri Gagarin became the first man in space on 12 April 1961. He orbited the Earth once in Vostok 1 before returning safely to the ground. In contrast the US space programme started badly, with a number of high profile disappointments. America's slow start was an embarrassment and it prompted President John F. Kennedy to restore national morale by

Yuri Gagarin was the first man in space. Gagarin's flight in April 1961 was a great propaganda victory for the USSR, and Gagarin became a national hero. However, by the end of the decade the balance in the race for supremacy in space had shifted in favour of the United States.

making one of the most remarkable predictions in space race history. In 1961 he stated that the US would put a man on the Moon before the end of the decade. It was a bold claim, but it captured people's imagination, and it came true. Neil Armstrong became the first man on the Moon when he descended to the lunar surface from his Apollo 11 landing module on 20 July 1969.

Although the rivalry continued in the 1970s and 1980s, the United States had now pulled ahead in the space race and would not look back. Funding space exploration was an expensive business, one which the Soviets found increasingly difficult to afford.

Buzz Aldrin was the second man to walk on the Moon. Aldrin followed Neil Armstrong onto the lunar surface after their historic landing on 20 July 1969. As their Apollo 11 *Eagle* landing module touched down, the United States took a decisive lead in the space race.

HOW DID IT HAPPEN?

The Space Race

What were the real reasons for the United States pursuing the dream of space exploration? Different politicians had different perspectives. President John Kennedy explained it in this way: 'Many years ago the great British explorer George Mallory, who was to die on Mount Everest, was asked why did he want to climb it. He said, "Because it's there." … Well, space is there … and the moon and planets are there, and new hopes for knowledge and peace are there.'

President Lyndon Johnson took a tougher line: 'Control of space means control of the world. From space, the masters of infinity would have the power to control the earth's weather, to cause drought and flood, to change the tides and raise the sea levels of the sea, to divert the Gulf Stream and change temperature climates to frigid.'

Both US presidents quoted in Hugh Brogan, *Kennedy* (Longman, 1996)

3 The World Holds Its Breath

The USSR's problems in Poland and Hungary in 1956 had led to widespread criticism around the world. However, America was not immune from international condemnation either. Its role in a spying scandal and the attempted overthrow of another country's government caused the USA much public embarrassment.

The secret practice of spying became public news when an American U2 spy plane was shot down over Soviet territory on 1 May 1960. The pilot, Francis Gary Powers, was captured and imprisoned. President Eisenhower initially denied the plane's existence. However, Khrushchev had the incriminating evidence in the form of the wrecked aircraft and the captured pilot, much to the embarrassment of the USA.

America faced more problems when revolution shook the island of Cuba, which lies about 150 km off the south-east coast of Florida. In the late 1950s Cuba was ruled by Fulgencio Batista. Although Batista was a dictator, he was an American ally, and US businesses had invested a lot of money in Cuba. In fact most of the farmland and major companies in Cuba were foreign-owned.

Fidel Castro addressing a crowd in January 1959 after the dictator Fulgencio Batista had been forced to flee from Cuba. The CIA attempted to assassinate Castro on many occasions and sometimes the methods it employed were rather unorthodox. At one point it was hoped that a box of exploding cigars might prove effective. That attempt, like others before and after it, failed.

VOICES FROM THE PAST

Fidel Castro

Although America was not hostile to Castro in the beginning, it was still wary of him. As former Secretary of State, Dean Acheson, told General George Marshall:

'This fellow Castro really knows what he's doing. He is going to cause us some problems down the line.'

Quoted in Douglas Brinkley, *Dean Acheson: The Cold War Years 1953-71* (Yale University Press, 1992)

An armed uprising against Batista's regime, led by a lawyer named Fidel Castro, succeeded in overthrowing the dictator in December 1958–January 1959. Batista fled to the United States along with many other Cubans. Although America had lost an ally, it was not openly hostile to Castro as he was not a communist. However, the situation soon changed. In February 1960, Castro nationalized the oil and sugar industries. At a stroke American companies lost around a billion dollars' worth of investments. In retaliation the United States refused to buy Cuban sugar or to sell oil to Cuba. Russia immediately plugged the trade gap, bringing Castro's government and the Soviet bloc closer together. This worried America, as the idea of a leftist government so close to the American mainland was completely unthinkable.

The CIA wanted to tackle the situation in two ways. Firstly it tried to assassinate Castro; but all the attempts failed. The other plan was an invasion, but rather than using US troops to invade, the CIA trained and equipped Cubans who had fled from Castro's revolution to exile in the USA. The CIA believed that the people of Cuba would rise up and join the exiles when they landed on the island.

Cubans celebrate the defeat of the American-trained exiles after the unsuccessful Bay of Pigs invasion in April 1961. The failed coup was an embarrassment to the United States and helped to strengthen the relationship between Cuba and the USSR.

The CIA was wrong. Around 1,300 exiles landed from US ships on the south coast of Cuba at the Bay of Pigs in April 1961, but there was no popular support. Within three days Cuban troops had defeated the exiles. There had been too few fighters to stand a chance of success. Also the promised air support from the US was inadequate – and hastily withdrawn when things started to go wrong and other nations voiced their disapproval of the American action. Castro had defeated the United States and moved closer to the USSR in the process. America's nightmare of pro-Soviet neighbours on its doorstep was becoming a reality.

Confrontation in Berlin

The developments in Cuba were of great interest to Khrushchev, particularly the performance of new US president, John F. Kennedy. Khrushchev thought him too young and inexperienced for such a big job, so the Soviet premier decided to put him to the test – and Berlin was the chosen venue.

Khrushchev had already made it clear that he wanted Berlin to be a neutral city with any Western presence removed from it. He repeated these demands to Kennedy, with a veiled threat of war if his demands were not met within six months. Kennedy would not agree, though in private he did wonder if it was worth going to war over Berlin.

Berlin was, politically speaking, a very sensitive issue. Although the border between East and West Germany was heavily guarded, the border between East and West Berlin was not. People were free to move from one sector to another without undue hindrance. This was a significant issue for the East German government. East Germans were escaping through Berlin to defect to the West. Between 1949 and 1961 around 2.6 million East Germans defected in this way. The steady loss of so many citizens threatened the economic viability of the East German state.

Although Khrushchev was hinting at war, he had another plan. When West Berliners woke up on Sunday 13 August 1961, they found their city being surrounded by barbed wire. East Germany had closed the border between East and West Berlin, and for good measure ringed the outside perimeter of West Berlin, sealing it off from East Germany. Both sides mobilized tanks and faced one another across the wire. War seemed likely; it took some frantic telephone diplomacy between Kennedy and Khrushchev to defuse the situation.

For East Berliners, the situation was desperate, and many people made frantic attempts to get to the West. People jumped from buildings or tried to climb the wire. However, fleeing across the border got even harder later in 1961 as the wire was replaced by a concrete wall complete with watchtowers and armed guards. The Berlin Wall – a potent and physical symbol of the Cold War – had been built.

A woman attempts to escape from East to West Berlin in September 1961. In the period between the city being divided and the wall being built many escape attempts were made. Some streets of houses lay directly on the border between East and West. It was possible to enter a house on the Eastern side and exit the back of the house on the Western side.

aßensperrung
verursacht durch die
chandmauer

TURNING POINT

A city divided

When the barbed wire went up around their city on the night of 12-13 August 1961, the Berliners were caught by surprise. People found that at a stroke they had been separated from friends and family. Even some cemeteries were split in two by the barbed wire border. Anyone who had been visiting friends or relations in a different sector that night found themselves trapped. The Eastern bloc had effectively admitted that it could not compete with the attractions of the West. By building the wall it clearly showed how it meant to deal with the problem – by force.

East German soldiers lay the blocks that will form the Berlin Wall. West Berlin had always been isolated, geographically, from the rest of the Western alliance. The wall was a potent symbol of this isolation. The German sign reads 'Road closed because of the shameful wall'.

War had been avoided in Berlin, but it was not long before the superpowers clashed again, this time over Cuba. On 14 October 1962 a US spy plane took photographs of a Soviet missile site in Cuba. Practically all of the United States would be within range of these missiles. Khrushchev wanted missiles placed in Cuba in retaliation for US nuclear missiles based in Turkey, which were close enough to strike most Soviet cities.

Crisis over Cuba

Publicly Khrushchev denied that missiles were there, but Kennedy had the proof. Kennedy was faced with two difficult options. He could invade Cuba, but the likely result would be nuclear war. Or he could try to sort the situation out diplomatically, but there was no guarantee of success. On 22 October Kennedy appeared on national television to explain the situation to the American people. He also announced that he would be setting up a quarantine zone around Cuba. Any Soviet ship entering the zone would be searched.

When the quarantine zone was announced, Soviet ships were already on their way to Cuba, along with a number of Soviet submarines. Khrushchev warned Kennedy that the submarines would sink US ships if they tried to stop his

President Kennedy makes a television address to the American nation during the Cuban Missile Crisis in 1962. Television brought a new immediacy to breaking news stories making the public feel both more involved and more vulnerable in times of crisis.

VOICES FROM THE PAST

On the brink

Kennedy's tough tactics during the Cuban missile crisis were successful, but for a while it seemed that the inevitable outcome would be war – nuclear war. Then secretary of defense Robert McNamara remembers:

'It was a beautiful fall evening, the height of the crisis, and I went up into the open air to look and to smell it, because I thought it was the last Saturday I would ever see.'

Quoted in Jeremy Isaacs and Taylor Dowling, *Cold War* (Bantam Press, 1998)

vessels. The situation was impossibly tense as the Soviet ships approached the edge of the zone, but in the end they turned back.

Next, the United States demanded that the Soviet missiles must be removed from Cuba, or it would invade the country. Some Soviet generals argued that the missiles should be launched at America. Khrushchev, however, decided to send a letter offering to remove the missiles if Cuba was not invaded and the quarantine zone was lifted.

The next day, Khrushchev sent another letter demanding that America must remove its missiles from Turkey if the USSR removed its missiles from Cuba.

Kennedy chose to ignore the second letter and instead wrote accepting the terms of Khrushchev's first letter. At the same time Kennedy's brother, Robert, who was attorney general in his cabinet, met the Soviet ambassador. The Soviet Union repeated its threat to invade Cuba, but the United States also suggested, unofficially, that it would remove the Turkish missiles. The Soviet Union agreed to Kennedy's proposals, and war was averted. Nevertheless, both sides realized how close they had come to nuclear war and it had frightened them.

A US destroyer escorts a Soviet cargo ship carrying missile parts away from Cuban waters. The naval blockade of Cuba almost led to nuclear war. It was a high-risk strategy on Kennedy's part, but when Khrushchev backed down, it confirmed Kennedy as a strong and decisive leader.

The Cuban missile crisis had made Khrushchev look weak and this led to his being replaced as premier of the Soviet Union in 1964. However, Cuba was not his only problem. The Soviet bloc was suffering economically – the cost of the Cold War was crippling it. Citizens in the East European bloc experienced a worsening quality of life. For once-prosperous countries like Czechoslovakia, such a drop in living standards was hard to bear.

The Prague Spring

Inevitably the deteriorating conditions led to civil unrest. In 1966 there were student protests in Czechoslovakia and the bad feeling there continued until 1968. In 1968 the Soviets installed Alexander Dubček, who was seen as a popular and sympathetic politician, as head of the communist party in that country in an attempt to calm the situation.

Dubček was sympathetic to calls for change and pushed through a number of political reforms. Some press restrictions were lifted which, for the first time, allowed people to criticize their government. The government loosened its control over business and allowed trade unions to negotiate with employers. Czech people were allowed to travel abroad more freely. This blossoming of freedom in the Czech capital earned this period the nickname 'the Prague Spring'.

This policy of liberalization was not well received in Moscow. The new Soviet leadership under Leonid Brezhnev was apprehensive as to where it might lead and was in no mood to accept any threat to the Warsaw Pact. If they allowed these political changes in Czechoslovakia, then other members of the Warsaw Pact might seek to make similar changes too. Soviet tanks were sent to the Czech border.

In fact, Dubček was a loyal communist and had no plans to leave the Pact. However, when he invited the Yugoslav leader, Marshal Tito, to Prague, the Soviets became even more alarmed. It seemed as if Czechoslovakia might try to follow Yugoslavia's lead and become independent. On 20 August Soviet forces crossed the Czech border and headed for Prague. Importantly, the Czech government did not resist the invasion and instructed the Czech people not to fight against the invading troops. This prevented a repeat of the Hungarian bloodshed.

Dubček was taken to Moscow and made to renounce the reforms he had overseen. He was replaced as leader by a more Soviet-friendly politician, Gustav Husák. The message to Czechoslovakia and the rest of the Warsaw Pact was clear. Changes would be met with force.

After the Soviet invasion of Czechoslovakia in August 1968, Czech students demonstrate in support of leader Alexander Dubček in Prague, the capital city. Student demonstrations were a common feature of civilian unrest in the Soviet bloc during the Cold War years.

HOW DID IT HAPPEN?

The Brezhnev doctrine

?

Soviet leader Leonid Brezhnev justified sending troops into Czechoslovakia and Hungary in his now famous Brezhnev Doctrine:'When internal and external forces, hostile to socialism, seek to reverse the development of any socialist country whatsoever in the direction of the restoration of the capitalist order, when a threat to the cause of socialism arises in that country, a threat to the security of the socialist commonwealth as a whole – this already becomes not only a problem of the people of the country concerned, but also a common problem and the concern of all socialist countries.'

But the Czech people were shocked by the Soviet action: 'The Soviets had said for decades they were our best friends and our brothers. They came with an army of half a million to suppress our attempt at more freedom. They came to crush it.'

Leonid Brezhnev quoted in Geoffrey Roberts, *The Soviet Union in World Politics* (Routledge, 1999); Eduard Goldstucker quoted in Derrick Murphy, *The Cold War 1945–1991* (Collins Educational, 2003)

Soviet tanks patrol the streets of Prague in August 1968. The Soviet Union found this blatant show of force to be an effective tactic in order to keep unruly communist countries in line.

4 Conflict

While the Soviet Union was crushing insurrection close to home, America was facing problems further afield – this time in Vietnam. For a long time Vietnam had been part of the French colonial empire. After the Second World War the Vietnamese led by the communist Ho Chi Minh fought for independence from French rule. The French withdrew in 1954 and Vietnam was split in two. North Vietnam was under the control of the communists under Ho Chi Minh; South Vietnam was ruled by the unpopular, but US-backed, Ngo Dinh Diem.

Ho Chi Minh. This photograph was taken in 1945 when he was fighting for Vietnamese independence against the country's French rulers. He died in 1969 while Vietnam was still embroiled in a ferocious war against the United States.

Part of the ceasefire agreement was a provision for elections to be held in 1956 to reunite the country. Diem ignored the deadline, so North Vietnam resolved to unite the country by force. In 1959 communists already in South Vietnam were organized into a force known as the Viet Cong with the aim of overthrowing the Diem government. North Vietnam both advised and supplied the Viet Cong.

Diem's rule was a problem for the US. He was vastly unpopular with ordinary Vietnamese, and ruthlessly repressed his people. Such an unpopular leader might encourage sympathy for the communists. The US did not have to intervene directly though; a group of powerful South Vietnamese generals rebelled and assassinated Diem in a coup in November 1963. The generals maintained the fight against the Viet Cong, and the country continued to receive US military aid.

In private, Kennedy believed that the South could not hope to win the fight against communism. However, three weeks after Diem's death, Kennedy too was assassinated. The new president, Lyndon Johnson, was determined not to lose Vietnam – even if this meant all-out war with the North.

The War Escalates

In 1964, with North Vietnamese troops marching south to help the Viet Cong, the US claimed that its warships had been attacked by North Vietnamese torpedo boats in the Gulf of Tonkin. The US now had its reason to attack the North. On 7 August 1964 Congress passed

TURNING POINT
The start of the conflict

The United States felt it had to get involved in Vietnam because it feared that if Vietnam fell to forces of communism, then surrounding countries in Asia would be destabilized and might also topple to communism in quick succession. This was known as the domino effect. The US was so concerned by this threat that in 1965 it was willing to commit its own troops to shore up the South Vietnamese regime. America was thus drawn into the biggest armed conflict it had experienced since the Second World War.

the Gulf of Tonkin Resolution which gave the US government a free hand to escalate the war as it saw fit. The US started bombing North Vietnam and sent troops to the South to join the fight. By July 1965, more than 180,000 US troops had arrived in Vietnam. By 1968 this figure had risen to 540,000.

The US troops that arrived in Vietnam went with the support of their country, charged with the task of halting the spread of communism across Asia. They would probably have proved more than a match for any other army in open conflict. The problem was that the communists would not fight an open war. Instead they used guerrilla tactics – concealment, sabotage and lightning fast attacks – followed by a swift retreat into the rain forest.

Viet Cong guerrilla fighters on patrol during the Vietnam War. Despite America's superior technology, the communist fighters proved more than a match for the US troops by using concealment, ambush and knowledge of the landscape as weapons. Fighting in small groups, the North's guerrillas employed tactics that proved highly successful.

The US forces relied upon their technology to counter these tactics. They dropped defoliants on forest areas to strip away vegetation to deprive the Viet Cong of their hiding places, and bombed supply lines and towns. More bombs were dropped on Vietnam than on Germany during the Second World War. But the tactics did not work. The bombing campaign angered and killed ordinary Vietnamese, and merely strengthened the resolve of the North Vietnamese.

In January-February 1968 the Tet Offensive, a well-organized Northern attack on important towns in the south, even succeeded in carrying the fighting to the grounds of the American embassy in the southern capital of Saigon. The Tet Offensive failed to bring down the South, but it did have a major effect on the United States. The US government now had serious doubts as to whether the war could be won. There was also pressure from public opinion at home. This was the first war that was covered day-to-day by the media. People at home could see television pictures direct from the conflict. When the campaign was going badly, US voters saw it. The public mood began to turn against the war.

These feelings were strengthened by news reports that US troops had massacred more than 300 Vietnamese civilians in the village of

One of America's most powerful weapons was the Boeing B-52 Stratofortress bomber. Each aircraft could carry around 70,000 lb of bombs and B-52s were responsible for devastating large areas of North Vietnam. However, these strikes were of limited effectiveness against the elusive and determined communist forces.

My Lai on 16 March 1968. The grand ideals of fighting the evils of communism had been dragged down by the realities of war, and the public did not like what it saw. A new president, Richard Nixon, was elected in November 1968 and he looked for a way to get America out of the war.

Taking the Long Road to Peace

Leaving the war was a long process as peace talks went slowly. It was not until 1973 that the United States was able to withdraw all its troops, leaving the defence of the South in the hands of South Vietnamese forces. Two years later the North invaded the South. Without US support the country was quickly overrun. Vietnam had cost America billions of dollars of aid and more than 55,000 American lives – and in the end this sacrifice could not prevent the country from turning communist.

A member of the US 1st Air Cavalry division signals to a helicopter that is about to land in a field north of Saigon. The US army relied upon helicopters to help traverse the inhospitable Vietnamese countryside and to ferry troops and supplies quickly from place to place.

VOICES FROM THE PAST

The changing mood over Vietnam

Some historians argue that one of the reasons the Vietnam War ended as it did was a major change in the public perception of the war in the United States. In the early stages the American people generally supported the war. However, as time passed and US involvement in the war grew deeper, a hostile reaction to the war developed in the United States. A journalist describes a peace march of 300,000 people in 1971:

'Never before in this country have young soldiers marched in protest against the war in which they themselves have fought and which is still going on.'

John Pilger, quoted in Tony McAleavy, *Superpower Rivalry* (Cambridge University Press, 1998)

Whenever the USA came into conflict with a communist foe, such as in Vietnam, the American government always had one eye on the Soviets and how they would react. There was, however, another communist power of note – China. China had been communist since 1949 when, after a long civil war, the communist forces of Mao Zedong defeated the Chinese Nationalist forces of Chiang Kai-shek. The Nationalists had been supported with aid from the United States, but it was not enough to stop Mao. The communists took control of the country.

Communist troops take prisoners of war outside Shanghai in May 1949. The Chinese civil war lasted from 1927 to the end of 1949 when the communist forces under Mao Zedong eventually defeated the Nationalists and took control of the country.

China and the USSR disagreed about a number of issues, but the principle of Chinese autonomy lay at the bottom of these arguments. China did not like the way the USSR had treated Hungary or Czechoslovakia and was not prepared to be just another satellite state agreeing to everything the USSR decreed. The Soviets on the other hand demanded that a unified communist front must be presented to the West. With such differing attitudes, conflict was inevitable.

China Goes Its Own Way

In 1958 China attacked islands off Taiwan, the last stronghold of Chiang Kai-shek and the Chinese Nationalists, without telling the USSR first. As the Chinese action nearly brought the USA into a war to defend its old ally, it was of great concern to the USSR. Conflict with America did not bother the Chinese, who had after all already fought against US forces in Korea. China thought the USSR had gone soft – the USSR thought China was too extreme. The Soviets withdrew their expert help from China's nuclear bomb programme. China went ahead and built its own bomb, first tested on 16 October 1964, without Soviet help.

Disagreements over policies finally turned into military action in 1969. Old territorial conflicts stretching back to the late 1800s over the Russo-China border escalated into skirmishes and military engagement. The two big communist neighbours were not seeing eye-to-eye. This schism was skilfully handled by Nixon, who managed to diffuse world tension and bridge the divide with some accomplished diplomacy. In February 1972, he became the first US president to visit China. The meeting actually achieved very little, but the very fact that Nixon had deemed it necessary to visit China confirmed the country as a new superpower.

President Nixon visits the Great Wall of China with his wife Pat (right) in 1972. Although the presidential visit achieved little in real terms, photo-opportunities such as this provided great publicity for Nixon's history-making diplomatic mission.

This made the USSR eager to meet with Nixon – the thought of China and America becoming friendly was a serious concern. So in May 1972 Nixon became the first US president to visit Moscow. Important business was concluded there as the Soviet Union and America signed the first Strategic Arms Limitation Treaty (SALT 1),

TURNING POINT
The SALT treaties

The SALT 1 treaty did help to limit the numbers of ICBMs that the United States and the USSR could deploy in their defence. However, as many other types of missiles were not covered by the treaty, the overall effect of the SALT agreement was limited. Nevertheless, the very fact that the rival superpowers were prepared to sit down and talk to one another was a real turning point in the Cold War. A SALT 2 treaty was signed in 1979, but it was not formally ratified by the US Senate when the USSR invaded Afghanistan.

which slowed the pace of the arms race. The two superpowers also re-established trade links and a new era of more peaceful co-existence seemed to be on the horizon. This period when the strain on international relations eased is often referred to as the détente.

The détente turned out to be short-lived, however. The USA and the USSR found a new reason to disagree with one another, this time over Afghanistan. In 1978 a pro-Soviet government, led by Nur Taraki, was elected and signed a treaty of friendship and cooperation with the USSR. Taraki's government proved to be unpopular with the more radical Islamic groups in Afghanistan, though, and soon civil war broke out.

The war was a problem for the USSR; it could not afford to lose a communist partner. The Afghan government was asking for help, but the Soviets were reluctant to get directly involved in an armed conflict. The United States, however, was supplying and training the Islamic rebels, known as the Mujahideen.

Invasion of Afghanistan

When US spy satellites showed Soviet troops massing on the Afghan border in December 1979, US president Jimmy Carter asked Brezhnev if the USSR was preparing to invade. Brezhnev said no. The very next day Soviet troops went into Afghanistan. Brezhnev

Mujahideen fighters pose proudly next to a downed Soviet helicopter in Afghanistan in 1979. The United States spent a great deal of time and money training the Afghan rebels to fight the Soviet invaders.

claimed that they had been invited, but to most of the world it appeared that a Soviet invasion was taking place. Carter was furious and cut many of the trade links with the USSR. Détente was over.

For the USSR, the intervention was a disaster, comparable in many ways with the US experience in Vietnam. The Mujahideen fought a guerrilla war, using Afghanistan's mountainous terrain to their advantage. Although Soviet troops controlled the large population centres and the capital, Kabul, the rebels held much of the countryside.

The Afghan conflict caused another high-profile casualty in a completely different field – the Olympic Games. The 1980 Games were due to be held in Moscow. Carter announced that the United States would boycott the games and urged other countries to do the same. Although most nations ignored Carter's call, the Olympics were crucially damaged by the absence of American competitors. The celebration of sporting excellence was not graced by some of the world's best athletes. Relations between the superpowers were at a low ebb, and the Cold War was about to get even colder.

HOW DID IT HAPPEN?

The USSR changes its mind over Afghanistan

When the Afghan leader Nur Taraki first requested Soviet aid to help his communist government, the USSR was reluctant to help. It feared what the response from the West might be. 'The negative factors (of sending troops to Afghanistan) would be enormous. Most countries would immediately go against us.'

However, by the end of 1979, the position had changed. It looked increasingly likely that the Soviet Union might lose an ally and leave itself exposed: 'In this extremely difficult situation, which has threatened … the interests of our national security, it has become necessary to render additional military assistance to Afghanistan.'

The USSR had committed itself to fighting a war which many Soviets rightly believed it ultimately could not win.

Aleksei Kosygin, quoted in Jeremy Isaacs and Taylor Dowling, *Cold War* (Bantam Press, 1998); report on events in Afghanistan by Yuri Andropov, Andrei Gromyko and others quoted on www.cnn.com/SPECIALS/cold.war/episodes/20/documents/report/

Lightly armed Afghan guerrillas were used in a highly effective fashion against the better equipped Soviet army. As the Americans had discovered in Vietnam, small groups of fighters committed to a cause and fighting in difficult terrain can be effective against even the best armies in the world.

5 The End of the Cold War

In 1981 Ronald Reagan replaced Jimmy Carter as US president. Reagan realized that the economies of the US and the USSR were very different. The US was riding the wave of new technologies and the economy was blossoming. The USSR on the other hand was still primarily an agricultural country. Not only that, it also had an unproductive economy. The financial burden of the Cold War was crippling the USSR. It was having difficulty keeping up with American advances financially, technologically and militarily.

Reagan's plan to gain an advantage over the USSR was quite simple – the US would increase its defence budget. America was going to spend its way to victory over communism knowing the USSR had no hope of matching its expenditure. The budget immediately increased by over 30 billion dollars and new nuclear submarines and bombers were ordered. US nuclear missiles were based in Britain and

The Rockwell B1-B long-range strategic bomber was just one of the many new weapons developed in the 1980s by the USA in its bid to pull ahead of the USSR in the arms race.

TURNING POINT

Star Wars

The Strategic Defense Initiative was a critical moment in the history of the Cold War because it had the potential to change the shape of warfare for ever. The development of ICBMs had meant that one country could attack another from long distance without a soldier or pilot having to leave his base. Now the range of warfare was on the point of expanding to include space itself. Reagan's plans worried not only the Soviet bloc, but many people in the West too, who were uneasy about the prospect of an ever-widening theatre of war. The growing anti-nuclear protest movements were now joined by people voicing their concerns about taking the arms race into space.

An artist's impression of how the Star Wars programme may have worked as a space-based interceptor vehicle speeds towards impact with a nuclear warhead launched against the United States. Reagan's dream of intercepting nuclear missiles in space never became a reality.

Germany. Support was also given to anti-communist rebels in Nicaragua and the right-wing military dictatorship of El Salvador which was fighting left-wing guerrillas.

On the face of it, there seemed little point in increasing spending on new nuclear weapons when there were already enough warheads on each side to guarantee that any country involved in a nuclear war would be destroyed. However Reagan had a new, startling plan. It was called the Strategic Defense Initiative (SDI), and proposed that satellites and ground-based systems should be developed that could shoot down incoming Soviet missiles before they hit their targets. This futuristic approach to defence earned the plan the name Star Wars.

The plan alarmed the Soviet leaders. They realized that if SDI succeeded, the balance of power in the Cold War would swing firmly in America's favour. Tensions increased when NATO troops took part in large-scale manoeuvres in 1983. The USSR suspected that these were a cover for a real nuclear attack and immediately put its forces on standby. Nuclear war had not seemed so likely since the Cuban missile crisis of 1963.

The readiness of the USSR to retaliate worried Reagan. He too realized that war might have broken out. The stakes had been raised militarily, socially and politically and tensions were increasing. There were frequent anti-nuclear weapons protests in Europe, and – another sign that East-West relations were fragile – the Soviets boycotted the 1984 Olympic Games in Los Angeles. There was an obvious need for change. And change was on the horizon when Mikhail Gorbachev became the new Soviet premier in 1985.

Vice-President George Bush (left) and President Ronald Reagan (centre) point out the sights of the New York skyline to Mikhail Gorbachev in 1988. The mutual respect that existed between Gorbachev and Reagan went a long way to bringing the Cold War to an end.

A New Style of Soviet Leader

In 1985 Mikhail Gorbachev became the Soviet leader. He was a reformer who was keenly aware that the USSR was in a bad state. The economy was under severe pressure from ballooning defence expenditure, the standard of living of ordinary Russians was poor, and corruption was rife throughout the communist party system. There was much work to be done, so Gorbachev implemented a policy of *perestroika*, or restructuring. *Perestroika* called for less control of industry by the central government, which Gorbachev hoped would have the effect of making the country more productive. Unfortunately, the economy was in such a neglected and unproductive state that little progress was made. The lack of results left Gorbachev open to criticism from all sides.

Gorbachev found himself trapped between the old-fashioned Soviet communists who disapproved of the changes and the younger generation who wanted to see more reform. Defence expenditure needed to be cut to help the economy, and this could only be achieved by cutting back on missile expenditure and scaling down military operations in general. The USSR entered into new arms talks with the US as a way of cutting down the number of missiles it needed to keep in operation; and in 1988 Gorbachev decided that Soviet troops should be pulled out of Afghanistan. The Soviet involvement in the

TURNING POINT
The end of the arms race

Mikhail Gorbachev needed to bring an end to the arms race to give the Soviet economy a chance of recovery. With this in mind he met Reagan for talks in Geneva in 1985. The discussions failed to reach any agreement, but there was rapport between the two leaders. Further talks in 1986 seemed to be making progress, but again concluded without agreement. Finally in 1987, the Soviet Union and the United States reached a landmark agreement to remove all nuclear missiles from Europe, and to reduce the number of ICBM missiles deployed rather than simply agreeing on upper limits. The arms race was effectively over.

A column of Soviet tanks forms up as the USSR prepares to pull its troops out of Afghanistan. Military operations such as the invasion of Afghanistan cost the USSR a huge amount of money – money it could ill afford to spend on unsuccessful military adventures.

Afghan ended in 1989. Around 15,000–20,000 Soviet lives had been lost, 3 million Afghans had fled to neighbouring Pakistan and the country lay in ruins.

Later that year, in a speech to the United Nations, Gorbachev announced that the Soviet army would be reduced by hundreds of thousands of personnel. Over the next few months it also became clear that Soviet forces would not necessarily be sent to support the governments of other communist countries. This was a break from the principles of the Brezhnev Doctrine. No longer would Soviet troops intervene to quell uprisings in the Eastern bloc.

These announcements fundamentally changed the way that the communist world functioned. For years the Warsaw Pact had been held together by force; now the threat of military intervention was gone. Gorbachev had started the process that would bring the Cold War to an end. He had also, perhaps unwittingly, set in motion the downfall of the Soviet Union as a superpower.

VOICES FROM THE PAST

Glasnost

Along with *perestroika*, Gorbachev's policy of *glasnost*, or openness, revolutionized life in the Soviet bloc. The press had more freedom, criticism of the government was tolerated, and previously banned books could be read. *Glasnost* was the catalyst for change.

'*Without glasnost there is not, and there cannot be, democratism, the political creativity of the masses and their participation in management.*'

Mikhail Gorbachev quoted on the website www.emporia.edu/socsci/hansen/gorb

The reforms Gorbachev implemented were the catalyst for a series of remarkable upheavals across most of the communist world. In January 1989 the Hungarian government made it legal to form new political parties and it scheduled elections for the following year. As the last of the Soviet troops pulled out of Afghanistan in February, the Soviet troops in Hungary were preparing to do the same. The following month they left. In May, Hungary opened its border with Austria, cutting down the barbed-wire fences which had long separated the two countries. Many Eastern Europeans fled to the West through Hungary's open border.

Pro-democracy protesters gather in Tiananmen Square in China in May 1989. This demonstration was held in the centre of Beijing in front of the world's newspaper and TV media, but it was ruthlessly crushed by the Chinese government.

A Climate of Change

The rippling effects of change in the communist world reached as far as China. Gorbachev was visiting the country in May to try to heal the rift between the two communist powers. The talks coincided with massive pro-democracy demonstrations in Beijing. Huge numbers of protesters, most of them students, gathered in Tiananmen Square. Once Gorbachev had departed, on 3-4 June Chinese troops moved in and crushed the protest, killing more than 1,000 of the demonstrators in the process – all in front of the watching eyes of the world.

Meanwhile, a happier story was unfolding in Poland. For many years the country had been beset by serious industrial unrest. Striking workers had formed an organization called Solidarity to co-ordinate trade union activity and, under the inspired leadership of Lech Walesa, it had become so popular that the Polish government had had to resort to martial law to restore its power. Now, after months of talks between the government and Solidarity, free elections were to be held. Solidarity performed exceptionally well in the poll and by August a non-communist government, of which Solidarity members formed a major part, was in power.

The sense that the old order was passing away in Eastern Europe grew stronger and stronger. In October 1989 people took to the streets in East Berlin demanding change. As the demonstrations grew in size, Gorbachev suggested to the East German government that the border with West Berlin should come down. In something of a chaotic rush the border was opened on 10 November. East Germans streamed through the Berlin Wall in celebration, or tried physically to knock it down with hammers and chisels. The Wall, that most potent symbol of the Cold War, had fallen.

By the end of the year Czechoslovakia's communist government had also fallen in a peaceful revolution. Romania too saw regime change in December as a bloody uprising led to the overthrow and execution of its communist dictator Nicolae Ceausescu. The Iron Curtain had finally been torn down.

Germans climb the infamous Berlin Wall as the border between East and West Berlin is opened in November 1989. In emotional scenes that would have been unthinkable just a few months previously, friends and families were reunited after nearly 30 years of separation.

Germans celebrate as their country is reunited in October 1990. Reunification turned out to be a logistical and economic nightmare as West Germany sought to raise the standard of living of its East German citizens. So far, however, it has worked better than many people dared to hope.

Many historians claim that the Cold War ended in the autumn of 1990 when the USSR, along with the United States, Britain and France, agreed to the reunification of Germany. The fear of a strong unified Germany was one of the main issues that caused the split between the USSR and its former allies at the start of the Cold War. Now it was the issue that ended it. The United States assured Gorbachev that, militarily speaking, Germany would operate under the banner of NATO so the Soviet Union need not fear an aggressive, independent Germany.

The End of the Soviet Union

Of course, the reunification alarmed some people in the USSR and added to the tide of criticism directed at Gorbachev. The economic situation there had not improved and many of the Soviet republics that formed the Soviet Union looked enviously at the new freedoms being enjoyed by their former communist partners. Over the course of the year the republics of Lithuania, Estonia, Latvia, Ukraine, Armenia, Turkmenistan, Tajikistan, Kazakhstan and Kyrgyzia all either declared, or voted for, their independence. Gorbachev tried to prevent the USSR splitting up in this way with a mixture of force and reform.

In November 1990 Gorbachev proposed a new treaty between the Soviet republics, which still bound them together, but in a looser way

HOW DID IT HAPPEN?

The legacy of the Cold War

Now that the Cold War is over, has the fear that stretched all the way from school pupils to presidents disappeared as well? Is greater safety its legacy? Here is one view: 'The world is far safer for the Cold War's ending ... It is hard now to realize or recall it, but whole generations in our time lived with the fear that one crisis or another ... might trigger a nuclear holocaust.'

Not everyone agrees. Some argue that the superpowers' willingness to arm poorer countries has left a volatile global situation. Even Mikhail Gorbachev worries that the opportunities afforded by the end of the Cold War will be abused for political gain. 'I wish I could say (the world is safer) but I can't.'

Jeremy Isaacs and Taylor Dowling, *Cold War* (Bantam Press, 1998); Mikhail Gorbachev quoted on www.cnn.com/SPECIALS/cold.war/episodes/24/interviews/gorbachev/

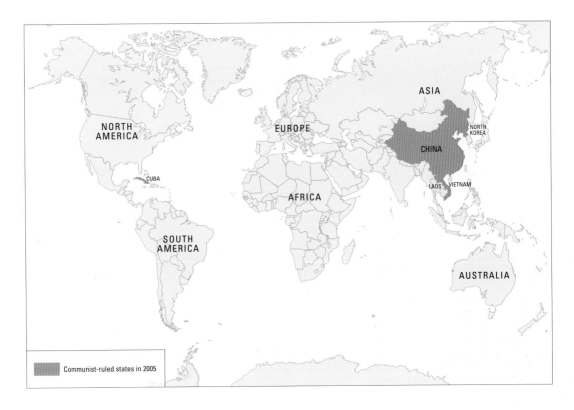

Communist-ruled states in 2005

than before. However, further unrest in Lithuania and Latvia saw Russian troops deployed and civilians killed. Gorbachev's attempts to appease both modernizers and the old guard with a mixture of reform and tough military action only succeeded in losing friends and gaining enemies. The proposal for the new union was voted in by a majority of the republics, but some of them boycotted the vote – a move supported by Boris Yeltsin, the influential leader of the largest republic, Russia. Gorbachev was losing his grip.

In August 1991, old-guard communists staged a coup and put Gorbachev under house arrest. They believed his reforms had gone too far. However, Gorbachev had given people a taste of freedom. A return to the old days was unattractive to the mass of Russians. Boris Yeltsin led the protests against the coup. Without the whole-hearted support of the people, and more importantly the army, the coup failed. Gorbachev was freed, but the balance of power had shifted towards his enemy and saviour, Yeltsin. Gorbachev resigned and his new union treaty was never implemented. Instead a new Commonwealth of Independent States (CIS) was formed – an idea championed by Yeltsin. All of the former members of the USSR, except the Baltic states of Estonia, Latvia and Lithuania, joined the CIS. By the end of 1991 both the Cold War and the USSR were consigned to history.

The political world in 2005 was a very different place to the one that existed in 1955 (see page 18). Europe was no longer fundamentally divided between east and west, and the number of communist-controlled states was greatly reduced.

Cold War Timeline

1945

4–11 February: Yalta Conference

17 July–2 August: Potsdam Conference

6 August: USA drops atomic bomb on Hiroshima

9 August: USA drops second atomic bomb on Nagasaki

14 August: End of Second World War as Japanese accept terms of surrender

1947

5 June: Marshall Plan announced in speech by George Marshall at Harvard University

1948

24 June: Berlin blockade begins

1949

4 April: NATO alliance formed

12 May: End of Berlin blockade

29 August: USSR tests atom bomb

1 October: Communist forces under Mao Zedong take control of China

1950

25 June: Korean War starts

1953

5 March: Joseph Stalin dies

27 July: Korean War ends

1954

March: KGB set up in the Soviet Union

1955

14 May: Warsaw Pact formed

1956

4 November: Soviet troops put down Hungarian uprising

1957

4 October: Sputnik 1 launched by Soviet Union

1959

1 January: Fidel Castro takes control of Cuba

1960

1 May: American U2 spy plane shot down over Soviet territory

1961

17 April: Bay of Pigs invasion of Cuba

13 August: Berlin divided

1962

16–28 October: Cuban Missile Crisis

1964

2–5 August: Gulf of Tonkin incident off coast of North Vietnam

1965

March: President Johnson orders US troops into Vietnam

1968

20 August: Soviet troops enter Czechoslovakia to put down government of Alexander Dubcek

1969

20 July: First Moon landing made by US Apollo 11

1972

26 May: SALT 1 arms limitation treaty signed by USA and USSR

1973

27 January: Vietnam War ends as peace agreement is signed in Paris

1979

25 December: Soviet forces invade Afghanistan

1980

20 July: Moscow Olympics start – the competition is boycotted by the USA

22 September: Solidarity confederation of trade unions formed in Poland

1983

23 March: President Reagan announces US Strategic Defense Initiative

1984

28 July: Los Angeles Olympics start – the competition is boycotted by the USSR

1985

11 March: Mikhail Gorbachev takes power in the USSR

1987

December: Reagan and Gorbachev sign Intermediate Nuclear Forces Treaty

1988

February: Gorbachev announces plans for withdrawal of Soviet troops from Afghanistan

1989

January: Soviet troops withdraw from Afghanistan

May: Hungary opens border with Austria

3–4 June: Chinese troops crush pro-democracy protesters in Tiananmen Square

August: Non-communist government elected in Poland

September: Hungary becomes independent

10 November: Berlin Wall falls

17–27 November: Revolution in Czechoslovakia

21 December: Revolution in Romania

1990

3 October: East and West Germany reunited

1991

July: Warsaw Pact officially dissolved

August: Attempted military coup in Russia

8 December: Commonwealth of Independent States formed as successor to the USSR

Glossary

atomic bomb A very powerful bomb in which an explosion is caused by nuclear fission – splitting the nuclei of atoms.

autonomy The right of a country to govern itself.

bloc A group of united countries.

blockade The act of surrounding a place to prevent exit from or entry to it.

boycott Refusal to trade with a country.

coalition A group of people, governments or countries united on a temporary basis.

communism A political system based on state control of the economy and people sharing wealth and property.

Congress The law-making body of the United States.

coup The overthrow of a government.

defect To change sides, to leave one country for another.

defoliants Weapons designed to kill the leaves of trees.

democracy A country where the government is freely elected by the people.

espionage Spying.

guerrillas Small groups of irregular soldiers usually fighting against a much larger organized army.

insurrection An uprising.

intercontinental ballistic missile (ICBM) Rocket-based weapon which can strike another country thousands of kilometres away.

Islamic From Islam, the Muslim religion which believes in the one god, Allah.

legacy What something or someone leaves behind after it or they have gone.

liberalization The process of becoming less hard-line and more open to change.

militants Aggressive, hard-line supporters of a particular religious or political cause.

propaganda Printed or broadcast information that tries to persuade people that a particular idea is good or that someone else's belief is bad.

quarantine zone An area where movement in or out is restricted.

rationing The act of restricting the amount of vital supplies, such as food or fuel, that a population can receive.

reparations Money paid by a defeated country to the victors to pay for repairing damages sustained during a war.

sabotage To damage or undermine something deliberately.

trade union An organized group of workers which operates to protect their rights and welfare.

United Nations (UN) A council in which each country in the world is represented.

veto To block a particular action, to refuse consent to something.

Further Information

Books:

Isaacs, Jeremy and Downing, Taylor, *Cold War* (Bantam Press, 1998)

McAleavy, Tony, *Superpower Rivalry* (Cambridge University Press, 1998)

McMahon, Robert J., *The Cold War – A Very Short Introduction* (Oxford University Press, 2003)

Montefiore, Simon Sebag, *Stalin: The Court of the Red Tsar* (Phoenix, 2003)

Murphy, Derrick, *The Cold War 1945-1991* (Collins Educational, 2003)

Websites:

http://www.bbc.co.uk/history/war/coldwar/index.shtml

http://www.cia.gov/cia/information/artifacts/index.htm

http://www.cnn.com/SPECIALS/cold.war/

http://www.coldwar.org/

http://mcel.pacificu.edu/as/students/Stanley/home.html

http://members.aol.com/veterans/warlib6x.htm

Index　Numbers in **bold** refer to pictures